Bruised Apples

Bruised Apples

Pamela Rawls

Lexington, Kentucky

BRUISED APPLES
Published by Pamela Rawls

Copyright © 2020 by Pamela Rawls

ISBN: 978-0-578-72482-9
Imprint: Independently Published

Nonfiction > Self-Help > Personal Growth > Self-Esteem
Nonfiction > Self-Help > Spiritual

Scripture quotations:
Scripture taken from the Holy Bible, NEW INTERNATIONAL VERSION®, NIV® Copyright © 1973, 1978, 1984, 2011 by Biblica, Inc.® Used by permission.

Cover design by Cierra S. Spaulding of Masterpiece Creative Group

Photo by Rob Morton

For more information:
Pamela Rawls
Email: authorpamelarawls@gmail.com

Dedication

I dedicate this book to my children. A separate "thank you" for each is definitely in order.

To my son:

You are truly an amazing young man. I have always tried to teach you to be loving and kind. You have given me what I have always tried to give you. You taught me that it was okay to love myself again and to take the time that I needed, so that I could find true happiness. I have watched you grow from a boy to a man. I have always been so strong for everyone else. Somewhere along the way, I forgot how to be strong for me. Your example of self-love reminded me how to do just that. You are the best son that a mother could ask for. I love you 3.

To my daughter:

You are me made all over, but better! You are the remix. The remix is always better than the original in my opinion. Not one person on this earth believes in my gift more than you do. You have been by my side since you were born. I laid you beside me in my hospital bed, and you have been by my side ever since. You once said, "Momma, you know what your problem is?" I, of course rolling my eyes, responded, "What's my problem little girl?" You looked me square in my eyes and told me that I worry too much about other people. You told me that it is okay to be a little selfish sometimes and to worry about myself. I love you so much for that. That, in many ways, liberated me. You are a confident, smart, strong, and beautiful young lady. I am so glad that God gave me you. You will always be my boo.

To Sweet Sadie:

Thank you for pushing me outside of my comfort zone. You would not let me give up on this book. I tried so many times to walk away from this project. You would not let me quit. You told me there were many people just like me in the world who needed my words. Thank you for watering my seed. You are an amazing sister. I will forever be grateful for our sisterhood.

To Clever Keyonna:

For the many times you pushed me; for the many text messages you sent; for the note you left on my car; for looking at me and telling me, I had a gift and I needed to share it; for reminding me a million times, I needed to finish this book - thank you. You were my driving force to complete this task. I love our bond and I do not take it for granted. From the pool to graduate school, we have been supporting each other. I love you my friend.

A big "thank you" to everyone who has loved, supported, prayed, and encouraged me. A special thank you to my sister circle. You ladies are everything to me. Thank you for always being exactly what I need! I love and appreciate you all.

~ *Pamela Rawls*

Contents

Acknowledgments

All of the glory and honor for this book belongs to God. He has given me the power of a sound mind and I am forever grateful for that. Along with Him, a few people deserve acknowledgment.

Thank you to my mother who has always been there for me. Thank you to my father who is resting with the Master. I love you both with a special type of love.

Thank you to my church family. You have loved and supported me through it all.

To my sisters. You hate to call names because you might forget someone. Markisha, I love you for always being my best friend. Paulette, we have been through a lot together. We are walking each other home. Isabelle, you are my ride or die. I have always said, "I don't even want to be on the planet without you." Jena, thank you for being the loving kind spirit that you are. Thank you for always praying for me. I love all of my sisters/friends from a special place in my heart. You all have been there for me through the hardest times of my life. Thank you for supporting, accepting, and loving me.

To the Reader

I want you to take your time with this book. Have a moment with the most important person in your life - you! You are everything. Put down all of the emotional baggage.

By the end of this book, I hope you are able to give your story a voice. I want you to do what I call "Speak Your Truth". While speaking your truth, you will be asked to respond to some questions. It is up to you to be honest. You will never heal from what you refuse to acknowledge. There will be times in this book you have to reflect on your pain, go into your emotional closet, dig deep, and pull out everything that hurt you. Do not worry. We are going to walk together - step by step - and chapter by chapter. The most important part of this whole process is that you speak your truth!

At the beginning of each chapter, I will give you what I call an "Apple Seed". Meditate on these seeds. Use them in a way that benefits you and your growth. Keep in mind that apples come in similar shapes, but different sizes and various shades of red. Apples can be sweet, tart, crisp, crunchy, spicy, tangy, juicy, smooth, firm or rich. There are many types, but they are all apples. Likewise, there are many types of women.

At the end of the day, we are more alike than different. I do not know which type represents you. I do know that even the best apples have bruises.

x

Introduction

Honey, you are everything! Once you believe that, the world will believe it too. It is my hope that by the end of this book, you will love everything about yourself. You will learn to embrace your flaws and everything else that you do not love about yourself. Whenever I see people living and loving their lives, it in return gives me life! The moment you realize that you are enough is one of the most monumental moments of your life. Acceptance is a huge part of that process. Happiness in itself is a process. If you take the time and do your Self-work, true happiness will be your result. The key to that happiness is realizing that it starts and ends with you.

Other people cannot make you happy. You have to give that gift to yourself. If you can forgive yourself, love yourself, and accept yourself just the way you are, it will happen. The real question is, do you want to be happy? Are you willing to do what it takes? It will not be an easy process. It may uncover some things that you thought you were over years ago.

I know what unhappiness feels like. I know how it feels to release an endless stream of tears. Emptiness and frustration became my best friends at one point in my life. After emptiness and frustration showed up, a few of their friends joined along.

I was in a marriage that took a turn for the worse. At the time, there was not anything worse than being married and feeling alone. I needed and wanted to escape this shallow place. I wanted to be in a place where only happiness existed. Was that even a possibility? You need to know that you are not alone!

Like so many other people, I was a slave to my imperfections. I was constantly making withdrawals from my love account to bless other people. Once I realized that there was no one making deposits - not even me - reality set in. It amazes me how much we give out on a regular basis. It becomes second nature. When pouring from an empty cup becomes the norm, feeling negative, empty, and depleted is bound to be the result.

How did I end up here? What was it going to take to reclaim my happiness and take control of my life? What happened to me, and all of the things that I cared about in life? Those were the questions that I started asking myself.

Day after day, I was stuck in a rigorous routine that I was a part of creating. I was completely lost. After working all day, trying to attend every extracurricular activity, and being "Wife of the Year", I was completely and utterly lost. I was beyond exhausted. My self-worth had diminished. My weight was out of control. Who had time for the gym? Yeah, right! I was no longer living; I merely existed. I had no personal stability. I did not love myself. Everything I had belonged to everyone else, especially my time.

Pause...nope this ain't going to work, sis! That is what I told myself. Get it together! I forgot who created me, which was totally insane, seeing how I was a faithful member of my church. How could I forget my weekly lessons about love, forgiveness, and grace? Well, I did. I forgot that Christ thought about me. He thought I was so special He gave up His life just for me. He thought I was worth dying for. If Christ thought enough to die for me, surely I could find the courage to live for Him. After all, I was created to be a living sacrifice.

At that point, I knew two things. First, I refused to live one more day for everyone else. Secondly, I knew God for myself.

I did not need anyone to tell me to read a self-help book. I did not want to hear, "Honey child, that's just a part of life!" The devil is a lie! I only got one life and I refused to give any more of it away. I refused to have another "moment". You know, that moment where you completely lose it and everyone acts as if you are crazy. There was no way that God wanted me to live this way! I mattered. My life mattered. My happiness mattered!

It was during that moment I was reminded of Isaiah 64:8, God is the Potter and we are the clay. It is His job to create us into what He wants us to be. My new prayer was, *God, you are the potter and I am the clay; do your thing!*

Have you ever seen a pot being molded and shaped? The potter starts with a lump of clay. Yeah, I am referring to you. The wheel starts to spin and the whole time the potter is in control. That part is your life going around in what may seem like endless circles. Water must be added. Those, my dear, are the many tears that must come. You see, they shape you into who you are going to become. God already knows how the story ends, but you do not. He takes His time, and shapes and molds the clay into what He wants it to be. Did you catch that? The clay does not make the decision, the potter does. Let the Potter do His job.

While you are on this journey called life, good things and bad things will both happen. We all know it is all about perspective. We have to be mindful that it is in the bad times when we will really see God do His best work.

My favorite parable in the Bible (in my own words) is when Jesus is on the boat. A terrible storm comes while Jesus is asleep. The disciples go crazy, wake Him up, and tell Him that they are afraid. The best response ever comes from Jesus. He says, "Why are you afraid? I am right here!" That story gives me life!

Don't you understand that during the storm of your life, Jesus is right there? He may seem like He is asleep, but He is right there. Trust Him and trust the process!

One of the hardest things that I had to do in my life was figure out who I was. When you are everything to everyone except to yourself, you never take the time to learn you. It is not because you do not want to; it is because your time has been spent doing for others. Figuring out who you are is never an easy process, but it is definitely a process worth fighting for every day.

Many times, I have felt alone. We are never alone when we learn to love ourselves because God is love. God is a very important part of my life. I chose to incorporate Him into this book because without Him I never would have made it. I have incorporated scriptures throughout this book. I refer to the scriptures as spiritual food. The same way I feed my physical body, I try to feed my spiritual body. Feel free to grab your Bible as a reference or a resource. Sit back and relax. Give your voice life. Take your time with each chapter. My best advice, if you want to be free from your personal bondage, then you must be honest and vulnerable when you speak your truth.

CHAPTER ONE

Walk with Me

Letting go and walking into your new season will be one of the most rewarding things you will do! You cannot have clarity about who you are if you focus on who you were.

Walk with Me

I am in no way a psychologist. I am not a marriage counselor. I am simply a woman who has been around for a few moons. I am only speaking from my life experiences. So, I am going to take you on a walk. As we begin our walk, I want to talk about your past and mine. The past can have a lot to do with who you are. You really have to be honest with yourself and open the closet door. You do not have to share with other people what is in your closet. This will only work if you are honest with yourself first.

What was your moment? What was the moment that happened to you that put you in the image category? The image category is that place where you realize how imperfect you were. It is the place where the spotlight shined on your imperfections. My moment was in the fifth grade. A boy told me that I was fat and I believed him. It changed some things for me and in me.

We were at recess and every boy had to choose a girl. I was the last girl left. The last boy was fire hot because I was his only choice.

He said, "I'm not picking her. She's fat."

My heart stayed on that playground for years. It was not that he said it; it was that I believed it. I fell in love with God at a very young age, but I still never thought I was enough.

It is not what someone says about you; it is what you choose to believe. Take your power back from that moment. Reclaim your power. Pull that root out from your garden. You will not be able to do it if you do not identify that moment.

The first lesson, do not let people plant negative seeds inside of you. If you allow that, the many tears you will cry will allow those seeds to grow and become rooted. After believing that I was not enough and that I was fat, I never thought that I would find real love.

I found what I thought was the love of my life. I was beyond happy. I found myself in a marriage that was my normal. My dad left my life for drugs at a very early age. My mother was both parents. That was a blessing and a curse. It was a blessing because it taught me how to be a strong, powerful woman. The down side to that was that it made me feel like a man. Trust me. I am all about equal rights! I was not soft or warm. I had the mentality that I did not need a man. I could do it all by myself.

Now, I still believe that a woman can do anything by herself, but you cannot be in a marriage by yourself. In marriage, love and respect are to be given mutually. If reciprocity is not in your love recipe, your marriage dish may not turn out the way you think.

Life, if you think about it, can be both amazing and traumatic. The best part about it is that we control our own narrative. We have the power to accept or deny. We have the power to laugh or cry. We obtain power! You have much more power than you are aware of. The power of life and death are in your words. Everything that you believe about you is true.

Think about this. We are all going to die someday. No one leaves here alive. Ultimately, we are all just walking each other home. While we are walking, I want you to let your past go and choose to wake up differently. The universe has chosen to allow you to be a part of this wonderful place again today. If God still wants you here, you have to be here both physically and mentally. You have to learn how to live and be present.

At times, life can seem a bit unfair. It can seem as if you have been buried alive. I am here to tell you that you have not been buried; you have been planted. You only bury what is dead. Even the Bible says to let the dead bury the dead. You are not dead in any way. You are very much alive.

We get so good at routines. We forget our own feelings and our own dreams because that is what we have become used to doing. We get caught up in our normality; we forget that we were placed here for a purpose. God has plans and a purpose for our lives. If God is for you, it really does not matter who wants you to fail. When the universe is on your side, it does not matter who is not! Waking up differently is a choice. Wake up speaking life into your future.

The Bible says the only thing following you is goodness and mercy. It has says, surely goodness and mercy shall follow you all the days of your life. There is a reason that the rear view mirror is so small and the windshield is so big. What is behind you is so much smaller than what is in front of you. Life is meant to be lived.

Many times, we provide the very opportunities that caused our misery. Think about the amount of toxic people you have in your life. Why are they welcome? Why do we give "First Class" seats to "coach" acting people? It is okay to let go of what or who is holding you back. It is okay to want more for your life. Your past situation is just that. That situation is not your destination. If you never let the past die, how are you going to live? Your past can seem like a prison with no bars.

Write in the Speak Your Truth section, the things that you really want to get off your chest. Write down all of the toxic things in your life. Writing is freedom. Write your truth, and be free.

Spiritual Fruit

Jeremiah 29:11 - For I know the plans I have for you, declares the Lord.

Luke 9:60 - Let the dead bury the dead.

Psalm 23:6 - Surely goodness and mercy shall follow me all the days of my life.

Proverbs 18:21 - The tongue has the power of life and death.

Ephesians 3:20 - God has more in store for you than you can even imagine.

Speak Your Truth

During this walk down memory lane, what was your most powerful memory and how is this still affecting your life? The more steps you take, the closer you will be to your destination. How can you walk into your new season? What will it take to let go of your past and your pain? Letting it go does not mean that it never happened or that it did not hurt. It means that you are choosing to live past the pain. What will it take for you to let it go? We all must remember that everything we choose is a decision.

____

____

____

____

____

____

____

____

____

BRUISED APPLES

CHAPTER TWO

Forgiveness

Here is the thing about forgiveness. The key is not to focus on them or what they did. Try focusing on who God has created you to be. Who knows how high you can fly without being held down!

Forgiveness

Personally, I had to start with forgiveness. I had to forgive myself. I wanted to blame so many people for my sad days. For me, it was feeling as if I was not enough. I was my own biggest enemy.

Once you start doing your Self-work, you will realize that people can only do to you what you allow them to do. A seed cannot be planted unless the soil is loose. Learning to keep my mind firm and focused was a huge part of my own growth. If you allow people to plant the seeds of doubt and unhappiness inside of you, it will surely grow.

It was not until the age of 30 that I realized that I was a huge part of my own pain. I chose to believe everything negative said about me. I gave up my power willingly because I did not think I had the strength to fight.

I suggest writing yourself a letter. Start with admitting to everything you allowed. I want you to speak your truth. This is not to pull the scab off a possibly healing wound. This is so that you can acknowledge your pain. Acknowledge your part and move on. In order for you to truly forgive yourself, you must identify it, forgive yourself, and let it go in every way.

We all have an expiration date. Admit that you have given enough of your life away so that you will not waste anymore of your precious time on things that you do not have the power to change. Holding on to something for too long can only cause you great pain.

I remember my dad from when I was a small child. I was a daddy's girl in every way. I was only about six years old when my parents got divorced. My dad became hooked on drugs. Initially, I did not understand what was going on. All that I knew was that my heart was lacking the presence of my father. As the years went by, I saw my mother take on both parental roles. A lot of my strength comes from her.

As a teenager anger set in. What girl wants to walk on the homecoming court with a man that is not her father? Let's not mention the hollow feeling that came when I walked across the stage to receive my high school diploma and his chair was empty. It is funny how we get used to pain. Then came my wedding day. You guessed it. He missed that special event as well.

In November 2002, my first child made his entrance into the universe. I thought for sure the birth of my dad's first grandchild would have made him want to get clean and be there. It didn't. I had a hole in my heart that material things could not fill. Only the love of my father could fill that gaping wound that seemed only to increase as the years rolled by.

More time passed and I was at the point where my college experience was ending. I reached out and asked him to come to my graduation. He promised me that he would come. He even asked what I would like for a gift. I did not want to get excited about it because if there was one thing that my father would do, it was to let me down. Now, let me be clear. You have to understand that people can let you down and still have only good intentions. The sad part is that your heart does not understand that reality. Pain still shows up when the one you love does not.

But, this time, he showed up! He came! He kept his promise to me. He even bought me my first digital camera. I still have that camera. It is not worth anything to the world, but it is worth the world to me. It does not have the capability to capture the amount of joy he brought to my life by simply keeping his word. However, over the years, he started to fade in and out of my life again.

A few years ago, I stopped to see him on my way home from vacation. I did not realize that day would be my last hug from my first love. I was devastated. The amount of pain I felt was unbearable. It felt like an elephant was sitting on my chest. There are days when the pain reminds me that it is still there. I am convinced the pain will never subside 100 percent. I am not sure it is supposed to go away.

This lesson in forgiveness is real. The saddest part of this whole love story is about forgiveness. I spent so many moons praying and wishing for my father to change - hoping that he would see that he was missing so many wonderful things in my life. When he passed, I was still hoping and wishing. I hoped that God would grant my wish. I still wish he could come back. I wish that I could have loved him for who he was. I wish that I did not spend so much time thinking about myself…and how he had let me down. I had to forgive myself for not being the best daughter to him. Sometimes, we become so focused on people not loving us, that we forget that God wants us to love them. Forgiveness is never for the other person. You do not have any control over them. You barely have control of yourself. It is best to let go of the things that are holding you back. It is a lot easier to fly without extra weight! Let it go, sis. Forgive them and forgive yourself. Note to self: forgiven people should always be forgiving people!

Spiritual Fruit

Isaiah 43:18 - Stop dwelling on the past.

Romans 12:17-19 - Release them from your punishment.

Matthew 5:44 - Pray.

Speak Your Truth

What is forgiveness to you? What are you holding on to that is keeping you from forgiving? The very thing that you are holding on to could be the very thing that is holding you back. God has forgiven you. It is okay for you to forgive you. You must remember that forgiveness is for you. You are worth it!

____

____

____

CHAPTER THREE

Having Expectations

You will gain serenity the moment you give up your expectations for acceptance. Before you can accept others, you have to be able to accept yourself.

Having Expectations

Insanity. What is the best way to describe this word? Have you ever done something over and over again, thinking that it would result in a different outcome? Yeah, me too!

Placing expectations or having expectations is something that just happens. We have a fantasy that if we give or do more for others, in return, people will respond the same way. When it is not returned, hurt and disappoint find a place inside of us. When you have expectations, you believe that something is going to happen or that it should happen. I have driven myself insane with expectations.

The moment that I relinquished the mere thought of having expectations, was the moment I could focus on the rose and not the thorns. I have always had expectations. I just did not know what they were. Here I was, a girl without her first love. I expected my father to be there for me! I expected him to work things out with my mother. I expected him to choose me over his addiction. That led to a lot of heartbreak, anger, and pain.

I expected to be treated like everyone else in fifth grade. It did not matter that I was bigger than all the other girls were. My mother told me that I was beautiful and I believed her. I expected everyone else to see me as my mother saw me. The boy in the fifth grade who told me I was fat, he also had expectations. That might have been the first time I realized that people will place expectations on you. You see, he expected to get the girl he wanted, and she was not me. It is not always what someone says, it is what you choose to believe. I chose to believe the boy over my mother. I chose to believe that my father loved drugs more than he loved me. That was not the case, but that is what I chose to believe. Life can put some heavy things in your hands, but you do not have to choose to hold it.

A wise woman once told me, "Pammie, don't ever have expectations. If you don't have any expectations, you can't be let down."

Honey, listen. That was the best piece of advice that I have ever received. That is a fact! Expectations only led me to a broken heart. If you really stop and think about it, who are we to expect someone else to do something? Expectations and acceptance are two very different things. Expecting my father to choose me only led to many sad days and many wet pillowcases. Now, if I had accepted the fact that he had a sickness or rather an addiction, it would have allowed me to direct my anger to the right place. At the time, I did not understand that, so the anger set up living arrangements in my heart. Every time I would think that I was over the pain or hurt, something would trigger me. This was a major clue that I had not dealt with heartache. It was buried or, better yet, ignored. The truth is we know when something triggers us. I didn't want to admit to it. I was afraid of how that would make me look.

Usually in life, things never end how they begin. A prime example is my marriage. I found the most amazing man on the planet. He was thoughtful, sweet, and kind. He always made me feel like I was the most phenomenal woman on the earth. However, over time, the butterflies left and the norm set in. The thing about the norm is that everyone's is different. What was normal for me may not be normal for you. I found myself feeling lonely, sad, and empty. Where was my knight?

Where was the guy who had swept me off my feet? It felt like he swept me off my feet and then handed me the broom. What were his expectations? Had I let him down in some way? Had I developed expectations without even noticing? We both did.

Without words, both of us had placed expectations on one another. We both lacked communication. Again, I suggest that you get comfortable with speaking your truth. Learn when and how to speak. Food cannot get inside of a closed mouth. Think about the areas in your life where you have placed expectations. Ask yourself why you placed them. Now, figure out how to trade them for acceptance. Let me be clear. You do not have to accept anything from anyone, but you also do not have the right to tell people how to be. You cannot change people. Think about how hard it is to change yourself. If a person wants to have multiple relationships, let them. You cannot stop them. Accept that it is who they are.

Adults are aware of their behavior. Are you aware of yours? You always have a choice. Might I implore you to choose yourself? The thing I love about God is that we can go to Him in expectation and know that He will fulfill His promise to you. He is not like men. His ways are not our ways. You can expect the great from God. He cannot lie; it is not possible. If you surrender your life to Christ, you will realize the plans God has for you are bigger than you could even dream of for yourself. Mighty are the works of His hands! Remember, He is the Potter and you are the clay. While the potter is shaping the clay, it is not an easy process. Accept what is and what will be. Let go of your expectations of man. If you can do this, you will have a lot less disappointment in your life.

Spiritual Fruit

Ephesians 3:20 - God can do exceedingly, abundantly, above all we ask or think.

Psalm 62:5 - My soul waits silently for God alone, my expectation is from him.

Hebrews 6:15 - And so it was that she, having waited long, endured patiently. She obtained what God had promised.

Speak Your Truth

What are your expectations for yourself and for your future? What are some of the expectations that you have placed on other people? How can you exchange expectations for acceptance?

BRUISED APPLES

CHAPTER FOUR

I Had Enough

Do not break down before your breakthrough. You have what it takes. You are more than enough. Stop trying to convince the world of your greatness, convince yourself! An oak tree starts out as an acorn. Everything you are supposed to be is already inside of you. You are enough!

I Had Enough

I have had enough! I want you to physically open your mouth and say those words. It is okay to give your thoughts a voice. When you are everything to everyone, it can leave you depleted. There comes a time when you have to start being everything to yourself. How do I start? How do I do that and not feel selfish? I am so glad that you asked me.

We teach people how to treat us. We position ourselves to say yes to everything and before you know it, everyone else's activities fill our days.

I remember waking up mad one day. I was upset because I had awakened in the first place. It is a very sad day when you do not want to wake up. Many people who contemplate suicide. I was not one of those people. I did not want to take my life, but I also did not want to go on living in this situation.

I remember going to church one Sunday. I did not enter God's house with thanksgiving. I entered with a selfish, miserable attitude. I was angry with my husband. The weekly task of having to get our children and myself ready were taking a toll on me.

I literally remember standing in my mirror thinking, *How is it that I can get three people ready and he cannot even find his dumb socks?* I was just angry. When you are mad and full of rage you will want an explanation about everything. That Sunday, was a different kind of frustration. When you have small children, daily frustrations somehow become normal. Most of the time, I would be frustrated with myself because my children were just being kids. I could not see that because anger had my vision skewed.

I have had enough; I am leaving, I thought. I literally got up and left church. I left my kids in Sunday school. I knew that my husband would take care of them. I just had to get out of there. I felt like my fake smile was the heaviest thing in the room.

I got up and headed for the door. I knew that once I smelled freedom on the other side, I could breathe deeply. As I closed the door behind me, I started down the steps, but I did not get far. One of the women in my church, whom I adore, was coming in as I was leaving.

"Where are you going?" she asked.

"I'm out of here. I don't feel like being here today. I've had enough."

She looked dead at me, square in my eyes. There was not anything sweet about her at that moment. She said, "Get back in that church! God didn't tell you that this was going to be easy". She was right. God never said that.

God never said it was going to be easy, but He did say that He would never leave you or forsake you. He did say that He would be with you always. I know that life can be hard at times, but He never promised you that it would be easy.

Learning to trust the process will be one of the hardest things that we will ever do. Not knowing the future can be frustrating. Gaining clarity is such a jewel. When we can step back and see the bigger picture, the small things become obsolete.

Psalms 23 states, in part, that my cup overflows. Overflow means that there is more than enough inside the cup. Honey, you are the cup. God has provided the overflow. It is your choice to live in the overflow or you can live in your emptiness. You have more power than you know. Stop and take in a deep breath. You cannot see the air, but you can feel it. You cannot see God, but you can feel him. He is in that sunset that takes our breath away. He is the morning dew that dances on the roses. He is in that constant chirp from the sparrows that His eyes stay upon daily. He takes the time to remind us that we matter and that we are not alone. You are not alone. It is okay to get to a point where you have had enough. We have all been there.

I decided to go back up the steps that Sunday. I am so glad I did. I learned that day that I mattered. I learned that there would be days when it will be tough. God is tougher. God is inside of me, that makes me tough! You matter. Your feelings matter.

I do not know where your steps are located, but choose to climb. Do not give up on you. When you have had enough, remind yourself that if God is taking the time to feed the birds, how much more will He provide for me.

Spiritual Fruit

Psalms 100:4 - Enter into his courts with thanksgiving.

Psalm 46:1 - God is our refuge and strength an ever-present help.

Matthew 6:28 - Look at the birds of the air, your Heavenly Father feeds them.

2 Timothy 4:17 - The Lord stood at my side and gave me strength.

Psalms 23:5 - My cup overflows.

Speak Your Truth

Have you reached a point where you have had enough? What does enough look like to you? Everyone's measurements will be different. Do not compare yourself to your neighbors. You may know the type of car they drive, but you do not know where they have been!

____

____

____

CHAPTER FIVE

I Am Enough

You are what you believe yourself to be. You are what you speak. Now, speak.

Pamela Rawls

I Am Enough

The moment that you realize that you are enough is one of the most monumental moments in your life. As a child, you never realize that you are not enough until someone makes you aware of it. It amazes me how we continuously judge ourselves past adolescence. Unfortunately, society has played a major part in how people determine their self-worth. We all, in one way or another, wished that we were something else - whether it be thinner, darker, lighter, or taller. We might pay for a thinner waistline and bigger breasts. We might want the big lips and now the big bottom to go along with it. The saddest part about it all is that it still might not be enough! It will never be enough. Emptiness will always be the final result until we stop using the world's ruler to see how we measure up. God said that we are wonderfully and uniquely made. I am not supposed to look like you and you are not supposed to look like me.

Several years ago, I started diet number 5,791. This time I started it differently. My 15th wedding anniversary was coming up. Honey, I saw this dress and I just knew that this was my chance. I was going to be everything in this gown! I just knew if I worked hard and ate correctly, my dream body, you know the one on the videos, was going to show up! Finally, I was going to be the world's normal. After many 4:00 a.m. workouts and months of eating healthy, I had reached my goal. I ordered the dress. I had so much hope and excitement.

The dress came in…I tried it on…and I looked like Sponge Bob Square Pants! It was hideous! I laid in my bed and cried for two days straight. It was another notch in my "I'm not enough belt!" Toward the end of the second day, my then six year old came in my room and voiced her opinion.

"Momma, get up out of the bed and get over the dumb dress. Just go get another one. You're still pretty, Mommy!"

Wow...out of the mouth of babes! How could a six year old be more intelligent than me? It was all so simple. Just go get another dress. After that, I quickly realized, not everything is for everybody. I wasted two days of happiness over something so frivolous. I allowed that dress to define me. I had laid in my bed, replaying those negative thoughts in my head, telling myself over and over again how fat I was…how gross my body was…how I would never be enough.

Every day, you have to speak life over yourself! Every morning, if God has given you a new 24 hours, take the time to admire His work. He made you. Do not disrespect His creation. You are gorgeous. It does not matter what anyone else in the world thinks of you. It only matters what you think. You are enough. The moment that you realize you are enough, like right now, at this very moment you will be free. There is nothing worse than feeling trapped inside a prison with invisible bars. After my seed fed me with encouraging fruit, I found the strength to get up. I went and found another dress. It was not what I had my heart set on, but it reminded me once more that not everything is for everyone. What looks good on you may not look good on me. At the end of the day, we have to focus on what is important. That was five years ago. I can guarantee that none of my guests could tell you what that dress looked like. We can place such high value on things that really do not matter.

I understand that you may not have everything that you want right now. What I can tell you is that everything that you are supposed to be, it is already inside of you. Acknowledge your greatness right now! You do not need a special occasion to recognize your greatness. Every morning look at yourself and appreciate your body. You cannot be a flower and a weed! Love what the mirror is showing you. Do not spend another moment trying to achieve perfection. Here is a secret between you and me, perfection does not exist. However, you can be your own kind of perfect. When you discover your own perception of personal perfection, you will realize that you are amazing. You are only living up to your own expectations. Love yourself with expectation.

Spiritual Fruit

2 Corinthians 12:9 - My grace is sufficient for you. My power is made perfect in weakness.

Jeremiah 1:5 - Before you were born I set you apart.

Psalm 139 – You are fearfully and wonderfully made.

Speak Your Truth

This chapter is my favorite! At some point or another, we all have been at a point of comparison in our lives. That was then and this is now. Write down some positive affirmations about yourself. Go over this list every day until you believe what you speak. There is power in your mouth! Use your power. Start with "I am…"

CHAPTER SIX

Screening Station

Letting go is the same thing as being still. Let go of the wheel and allow God to drive. After all, He has already determined your destination.

Screening Station

Every morning, I check my Bible App. I read the daily Word and try to apply it to my life. On this particular day, the scripture was Psalm 23. The focal point was, He leads me beside the still water. I have read this scripture a million times. God is so amazing. He knew what He had in store for me that evening.

It is very hard to get me to be still. On the contrary, being still is one of the most important things that you will ever do. I have learned, it is in the still times that you will get the most clarity.

That day, I was in "Boss" mode. I had ten million things to do, and I had to get them done. It was one of those days where you realize that you cannot get mad at anyone about the amount of food that you have to eat because you fixed your own plate. I had put way too much on my schedule. By the time I got to work, I did not have anything left in me. I was completely exhausted.

It is amazing how God sets everything up! I had been placed at a screening station during the pandemic. My job, prior to the pandemic, was working in the cardiac cath lab. I took care of Neurology and Cardiology patients. While screening, every night, I was with a different employee. That night, I was placed with a very special spirit. It is very hard to get me to process the opinion of others. I have programmed myself to understand that everyone is different and is entitled to his or her opinion. What other people do and say are not my concern. However, there was something different about this woman. She spoke with certainty. After a brief conversation, I was certain that she was the still water that Psalms spoke of that morning. I spoke these words to my unknown co-worker.

As I threw my purse on my desk, I yelled, "I'm running to get a double shot of espresso! I'm tired, I'm struggling and I'm not going to make it tonight if I don't have it." I am sure she was thinking, *Who in the world is this crazy woman?*

"Umm…okay," was her mild response.

After consuming the liquid energy, I engaged in a full conversation.

"Girl, I'm so sorry. It's really been a day! My name is Pam and I usually work in the Cath Lab."

She gave me her name. We began to chat as if we had known each other for years. We had many things in common. After we conversed for a while, my only choice was to be still. We talked about marriage, children, loving yourself, grief, and choices. She asked me about my 20-year marriage. I told her that I had to make the hardest choice of my life - leaving the man that I loved. She asked me about the process, and how I came to that decision.

"It was the hardest thing that I have ever had to do," I responded.

You see, when you are uncomfortable in your comfort, you become complacent. I had gotten used to not caring about me. My feelings no longer mattered. My children, family, church, and friends had become my new thought process. The endless days of being lonely were overshadowed by the opinion of others. This is why I no longer value many opinions to this day. If you let them, people will place their unreachable expectations on you. Do not ever let some place their expectations on you. This is your life!

I finally got the strength to make the choice that was best for me. I did not ask anyone's permission. All I knew was that I deserved better. No one could define my better. That was my job. This life transition took me through grief, pain, sadness, and finally liberation.

The thing I needed to be liberated from the most was my own mind. My mind had me overthinking. I am and have always been way too analytical. The thought of me being a failure almost consumes me on a daily basis, even more so since I ended my marriage. Perfection and validation are the two things that I struggle with the most. One does not exist and the other is something that you should only get from yourself.

That morning, I read, "be still". I heard the same words in the beating of my heart as my co-worker spoke. Be still. I will not share everything that she and I talked about that night. However, I would be selfish not to share this. I told her that after much prayer, I chose to leave my husband. How would I ever know if I had made the right decision?

Her response was, "It doesn't matter if it's what's right. It only matters if it's what was right for you!"

Wow! Game Changer. Listen to me. If you do not get anything else from this book, get this. It does not matter what anyone thinks. It only matters what you think. If you are confused about what to do, be still. Be still and know that God is not like man. He cannot lie. His ways are not our ways. He will lead you by the still water so that you can see your way. The hardest part is learning to trust and learning to be still. Trust the process. We all want a photo finish. You will never capture the perfect moment by moving! Learn to be still!

Spiritual Fruit

Psalm 46:10 - Be still and know that I am God.

Exodus 14:14 - The Lord will fight for you, you only need to be still.

Psalm 23:2-3 - He leads me beside the still waters; He restores my soul.

Speak Your Truth

Ask yourself, "When is the last time I heard from God?" I would like to challenge you to start noticing signs in your life. Notice how God takes the time to speak to you through things and people in your life. When God speaks listen. Do not ever be so busy in life that you cannot stop and learn the lesson that He is teaching you. Learn to be still. I always say, you can either stop or be stopped. God has a way of getting your attention one way or another. If He is trying to slow you down, it is for a reason. Allow Him to lead you beside the still water. Be open to receive whatever it is that God will show you. What has God been trying to show you? What is something that keeps happening in your life, but you keep ignoring it? Allow this segment to be your screening station!

____

____

____

____

____

____

____

CHAPTER SEVEN

Your 'It'

Only put on your plate what you are going to eat. Do not allow other people to make your load heavier than it needs to be.

Your 'It'

The Dictionary defines motion as the action or process of moving or being moved. Isn't it ironic how in the previous chapter I encouraged you to be still and now I am speaking of movement? The act of being still is intended to last only for a moment. The Bible says, He leads me by the still water. It never says, He makes me stop by the still water. Life is full of waves and you will not always be in the same place. You have to want to get to a deeper better version of yourself. Once God gives you clarity to move, receive it.

Reception can be difficult at times. I know for myself I am great at giving, but I am terrible at receiving. A wise man once told me, as much as you pour out, that much needs to be poured back into you. This was a hard process initially for me to grasp. I thought because I am a Christian, it was my job to give out constantly. Absolutely not! This is not what God meant when he said be a cheerful giver.

Psalms 23:5 says, my cup overflows. God will give you more than you need. He will allow your cup to overflow. When your cup is more than full - give. When you are in lack, be open to receive. Pouring from an empty cup left me feeling empty and neglected. I would be remiss not to mention that it made me feel somewhat unloved. Let me explain the meaning of pouring from an empty cup.

When you have to give to someone, no matter the person, and you really do not have "it" to give. Because you have given so much to others, you have given of yourself until you are spent. You have pulled another rabbit out of the hat when the show is over. You have said, "Yes" when all you really want in the world is to say, "NO!" Now, you get to determine your "it". My "it" was my own self. I cannot blame others for my choices. I never said no.

"Pam, can you…?"

My response was always, "Yes" or "Sure." It did not matter if it was my friends, mother, husband, children, church or job. If someone needed my help, I felt it was my duty to keep my cape on at all times.

I remember being in school full-time. My husband and I were taking care of my dying father-in-law. It is important to mention that my husband worked the second shift. Yes, you guessed it! That burden fell upon me. Here I was taking care of him, my then 2 year old son, in school full-time, doing hair part-time, working full-time, doing all I could for my church, and all while trying to be the perfect wife. Yes, you guessed it; this plane was about to crash. All of that was a homemade recipe for an empty cup. Not only did I not have anything left to give, I had neglected myself.

One day I found myself not wanting to wake up. I did not want to kill myself; I was just okay with not waking up. I have never been diagnosed with depression. I am not sure if I was depressed. I was sure that I was empty.

I knew that I could no longer give away what I did not possess, only to people please. Let's call a spade a spade. Saying "yes" all the time is a beautiful form of people pleasing. Ultimately, you do not want to upset anyone. You do not want to carry the disappointment of letting someone down. The truth of the matter is, you are letting someone down every single time. Yes, you guessed it…you! You are letting you down. You are trading your happiness and peace for someone else's temporary satisfaction. I use the term "temporary" because it will not be long before they return in need of something else. It is never wrong in any way to help or give unto others. However, I believe that you should never give away what you do not have to give because you matter too. If it has been a bad day, know it is okay to say "no". The best part is even if it has been a great day, it is still okay to say "no". It does not make you mean; it makes you matter!

It is okay to run a bath for yourself, light a candle, and love on you! I do not think that we tell ourselves how important we are. Oftentimes, we treat ourselves the way the world treats us. Here is a secret, do not tell anyone. You taught them how to treat you. Switch that today. Make a major move today! Transition from the place of always saying "yes" to doing or saying what you really want to do. It will be hard at first, but the more you do it, the easier it becomes. Trust me; you will be better for it. If you want to be a better you, you have to want to grow. Growth is never comfortable. Allow me the opportunity to remind you that we were not created to be comfortable. Do not ever become content with complacency. You are on the journey of becoming your best self. You cannot create a new picture overtop of old artwork.

Spiritual Fruit

Psalms 23:5 - You anoint my head with oil; my cup overflows.

2 Corinthians 9:7 - God loves a cheerful giver.

Matthew 11:28 - Draw near to me. I am gentle and my ways are light. You will find rest.

Speak Your Truth

Only you can determine your "it". Do not let anyone else tell you what your capabilities are. You have the power of a sound mind. Now, this process will only work if you are honest with yourself. How often do you do things because you want to be seen in a certain light? How many times have you said, "Yes" when you really wanted to say, "No"? Do you know how to keep your cup full? Are you able to be receptive? Acknowledge your "it" to yourself, while you speak your truth. What are you going to do to empty your own cup? Now, how are you going to fix it? Come on, honey, Speak Your Truth!

____

____

____

____

____

____

CHAPTER EIGHT

So Much More

Life is good, but it can always be better. There is so much to life. Start expecting so much more.

So Much More

Mother's Day 2008 started amazing. I had gotten up and gone to church as usual. This Sunday was nice because my husband was joining me. Whenever he would come to church with me, it always made me feel complete. It was nothing better to me, than serving God together.

I was about eight or nine weeks pregnant. That was a real shocker because we had a four-year-old son. At the time, I was convinced that I did not want any more children. Imagine my surprise when I was late for my cycle. I was livid. I could not believe it! I was going to have to start all over with changing diapers and bottle-feeding. I would have to watch and listen to my husband snore, while many sleepless nights would soon be my life again. In some ways, I resented him for allowing me to get up night after night. The bags under my eyes were clearly never a clue to him that I was beyond exhausted. However, as every good mother and wife states,

"This too shall pass." This may sound incredibly insensitive to the women that cannot carry children, but stay with me.

Church service came and went. After the service, we went to my mother's house for a cookout. I started to feel cramps. This was weird; I do not remember having this with my first pregnancy. Typical me, I blew it off and just kept moving. After a while, the cramps become more intense. I went to use the bathroom and there was blood. I think, *Why is there blood?* I panic. I told my husband, and then I called my doctor immediately. She told me nonchalantly that I was having a miscarriage and nothing could be done to stop it. She said, "Go home, lay down, and come to the office in the morning."

We left my mother's house and I was a mess. The baby, you know the one I did not want, was in the process of leaving my body and there wasn't anything I could do about it. Initially, I did not want this pregnancy. Now, I did not want it to end. I remember laying in the bed by myself, losing that baby. That was one of the many times I felt so alone while being with someone.

The next day, I went to the doctor alone. I remember the tears tickling my ears as they ran from my eyes, but it did not make me laugh.

"The process is almost over," the Ultrasound Tech told me as if this was normal.

This taught me a very valuable lesson: the Lord gives and the Lord takes away. I told myself, the next time the Lord gives me a blessing I would appreciate it. I took my blessing for granted. There were a million women, who would have killed to have seen that plus sign on that stick. There I was pissed at the world because I didn't want to have another baby. The tears were unstoppable.

As I wiped my face, I knew something had to change. What happened to me? How did I get to a place that I did not want to bring another child into the world? Who was I or, better yet, who had I become? Those were just a couple of questions that I could not answer about myself. It was clear that I had lost myself. This was another instance where I had forgotten about me.

There has been several times in my life that I have traded myself for everyone else. This includes my children. On an airplane, they clearly tell you that in the event of a crash, place the air mask on your own face first. After you place the mask on your face, then you will be able to place it on the next person. That small lesson taught me that it is so important to take care of yourself first. It does not make you selfish to love and care for yourself. Once I started loving on me and being thankful for all of my blessings, big and small, abundance showed up.

Being a mother is the best gift that I have ever received. I love my children more than my own life. The bond that we share is everything to me. I am so thankful that God chose to give me another chance at being a mother.

A year later, I was blessed to bring a beautiful daughter into the world. Losing a baby was an indescribable pain. It made me feel as if I was less of a woman. It made me confused about who I was as a person. I know who I am now. Sometimes life has to teach us lessons. Again, growth is not comfortable. Life has reminded me that I am so much more. I am more than a wife, mother, daughter, and friend. I am a child of the Most High and He has plans for my life. Jeremiah 29:11 states, "For I know the plans that I have for you…" That is my favorite scripture in the Bible. Knowing that God has a plan for my life gives me life. It simply reminds me that being a mother is not my only job while I am here on earth. It is great to be needed, but you do not need to be great. You just need to be you. You are enough! It is He that has created us and not we ourselves.

Spiritual Fruit

Jeremiah 29:11 - For I know the plans I have for you, declares the Lord.

Job 1:21 - The Lord giveth and the Lord taketh away. Blessed be the Name of the Lord.

2 Timothy 4:17 - But the Lord stood with me and gave me strength.

Joel 2:25 - God can restore what is broken and change it into something amazing.

Speak Your Truth

This is your truth! No one gets to tell you about your feelings. I am giving you my experience. These are my feelings and my perceptions. Dig deep. You cannot bury seeds on the surface. If you want to see your life garden, you really have to go beyond the surface. Think of a time when the Lord had to remove something from your life. After it was removed, how did it make you grow? The book of Job is a great example of loss and gain. The Lord has plans for each of us. We have to trust the process. Trust the universe in every area of your life, even when dealing with loss. I am not saying that it will be easy. I am telling you that it will be worth it. Acknowledge your loss. Allow yourself the proper time to heal. Ask God what you can learn from it and how can it be used for his glory. You are so much more; there is so much more. Explore your losses, but concentrate on your gains.

____

____

____

____

____

____

____

____

____

____

____

____

____

____

CHAPTER NINE

Choices

It isn't the package that determines the blessing. It's what's on the inside.

Pamela Rawls

Choices

"He is so cute!"

Those were the words that I spoke to my best friend as I noticed this random guy. He never really noticed me, which was something that I was used to. It was common for the big girl always to be heard, but never seen. I kept bugging her to set us up on a date. This might have been the only time in life that she let me down. She never made it happen.

After exchanging numbers, we began talking on the phone for hours on end. A few months later, we ended up going on a date. He was sweet and very kind. We dated for about six months. After a month, we were in love. As the old saying goes, "First comes love then comes marriage, then we bought a baby carriage."

We had our share of 'ups and downs' like any marriage. We brought our first son into the world and it was nothing like what I thought it would be. I have always been the kind of person who has believed in reciprocity in every area of my life. I could never process why cleaning or cooking had to be my job. I would be fire hot angry if the household duties were not shared. Yes, you guessed it; I stayed angry a lot. Our constant argument would always be about housework and his lack thereof. In my mind, I could never understand why someone would rather argue verses engaging in teamwork.

From my perspective, that is what marriage is. You fall in love and you become a team. It is the two of you against the world. The sad part is that sometimes the world comes in and knocks you both down. If you cannot stand, you cannot fight.

We worked two different shifts. We went from teammates to roommates with a baby. According to him, he gave as many baths and fixed as many bottles as I did. I guess I am worse at math than I thought.

After a while, the heated discussions got old and instead of verbalizing my feelings, I started to allow them to become rooted. I have always been a communicator. I hate holding my feelings in. It is funny how you learn to do what you hate. I learned too, at times, to swallow my voice.

We both went back to college at the same time and were still on separate work shifts. At this point, we had a two year old. On top of everything else, his father was sick and needed to live with us. To his credit, he took great care of his father. He was a great man. My husband was a great man as well; he could just never figure out how to love me. I am not sure where the blame needed to be placed, or if the pain just needed to be recognized. By the time we had to say goodbye to my father-in-law, our son was almost four years old. We both finished school and had jobs in our respective fields.

At this point, the loneliness had become so familiar that I thought it was normal. "The fire always goes out," is what I was told. This did not feel like a fire going out. This felt like a mouse on a wheel. No matter how fast I would run or what I would do, our marriage stayed in the same spot. And, please do not mention the word divorce and be a Christian. You would think that you just committed the worst sin possible. I was present when I made my vows. I took them very seriously. I never wanted a failed marriage. Who enters into marriage with divorce being an option?

At that point quitting was not an option for me. This was the first time we tried marriage counseling. We finished our sessions. The more things changed the more they stayed the same. After the pregnancy happened, mentioned previously, that was my breaking point. After going through what felt like one of the worst times in my life alone, I decided to leave.

After a month of separation, he asked me to dinner and I went. He knew what to say and what to do to win me back. I felt God telling me to go back. That was probably the best moments of our marriage. We were blessed with a baby girl. For a while, life was great. More time passed and the fire was no longer a blaze. We entered back into the monotony of our world.

The second set of marriage counseling took place. We had a different counselor with the same issues. It is hard for a woman to feel like she has to do it all - work, take care of the children, help with elderly parents, be a wife, church, and the list goes on. Sometimes I would wonder if he married the couch or me because the two of them were inseparable.

Temporary change took place and the years were still passing. Emptiness and contentment somehow became a part of who I was. It felt so familiar. I had become used to feeling unwanted and lonely. I wonder if you can guess what came next...counseling sessions number three. At this point, I have already begun my self-work. I knew that there had to be something going on inside of me, especially if I had chosen to swim in a sea of unhappiness.

There is no end to this chapter. You see, we all have a story and this one is mine. It is still being written each day. I wanted to share this to enlighten you. I came to my breaking point several times. The heart and the head almost never agree. Now, your intuition will always speak to you. You have to choose to listen to it. Who knows where I would be if I had listened years ago. I chose to ignore my unhappiness. Instead of creating a genuine smile, I chose to perfect a fake one. My marriage was not all bad. We really had some great times. I needed more. No one can define my more. The moment that I decided to become my best self was the moment I decided that my happiness would be a priority and not an option. This journey has not been easy. I have had to make some hard choices. The best choice that I made thus far was choosing me.

Spiritual Fruit

John 3:18 - Let us not love with words or speech but with actions and in truth.

Isaiah 60:22 - When the time is right, I the Lord, will make it happen.

Philippians 4:6 - Worry about nothing and pray about everything.

Speak Your Truth

Only you know how real your smile is. I hope that you will be true to you and your feelings. Give yourself a fair chance at happiness. A lot of us spend way too much time trying to please others. What is your life story? Can you identify the area in your life that you are not being your best self. Do not compare your story to mine. We are all created differently. You cannot use my ruler to measure your happiness. Write down what makes you happy. What are the choices that you have made that you regret? Now, what are the choices that you are going to make in the future to ensure that you are on the journey of being your best self.

____

____

____

____

____

____

CHAPTER TEN

This Place

Saying goodbye is never easy. It is easy to become attached, even if it's not good for you. Learn to release so you will be prepared to receive.

Pamela Rawls

This Place

"You have to leave!"

Those were the hardest four words I have ever spoken in my life. When I asked my husband to leave our home, it took everything out of me. I loved this man. I loved my family. I felt selfish and liberated at the exact same time. When I decided to make myself a priority, I decided to go see a therapist on my own. I had been to counseling before, but it was always as a married couple. Therapy was not something that was, or is, widely discussed.

My whole life I have always had issues with my father not being there, my weight, and just knowing that I was enough. I tried many times on my own through prayer and other self-help avenues to find my way to a healthy me. I am a firm believer in prayer; let me be very clear about that. I truly believe that prayer changes things. I also believe God has given us the power of a sound mind. I knew in my mind, there were people who had professional training who could offer me help.

At first, I was ashamed of needing to see a therapist. I thought that I would be seen as weak. I am a strong woman who can save the world. What did I look like seeking help from an outside source? It does not matter how strong of an eagle you are, eventually your wings will get tired.

The first request was, "So tell me some things about yourself."

I made myself comfortable on the couch. What a loaded question that was. I knew what the world expected me to be. I knew who I was to everyone else. I did not know who I was to me.

"Well, I'm not really sure how to answer that question. I am a mother and a wife. I'm a lover of God. I work in the Heart Cath Lab. I love saving a life and almost cry every time I lose one. I'm a motivational speaker. I love to encourage and uplift people."

"Well, that's great," she replied. "Now, tell me some things about you. You just described the many roles you play." That statement alone was a Game Changer.

"Well…let me see. I'm a woman who feels empty and unloved," I began. "I give a lot. I love to give to people, but I have a tremendous time being able to receive things. I have been married my whole adult life. I love my husband, but I feel like our marriage has run its course. I feel like he is not into me. I am beyond tired of telling him what I need. I have lost a lot of weight and I still feel like I am a thousand pounds. I am stuck in a mental prison."

"Now, we're getting somewhere. What made you want to come see me?" That was her second question.

My response was simple, "I can't do this on my own. I've tried several times on my own."

I never knew my invisible cape had limitations. No one has ever told Batman that he is not real. How do you handle finding out that you are the hero and the villain? How can you be your biggest cheerleader and your worst enemy at the same time?

After several sessions, I felt like I had been freed. Prior to starting therapy, I had begun my work. I had taken the time to collect the puzzle pieces. I am so thankful she helped me to solve it, so I could see the entire picture. I am the picture. All of these pieces that I was carrying around were parts of me. There were things that I needed to let go of from my past. There were things that needed to be cherished. I had to spend some time forgiving some people along with myself. The thing I had to do the most was accept what was and be strong enough to let go of what could never be.

I would never be a size two with a perfect body. I had to accept that. Accepting that meant accepting that I was a beautiful woman inside and out just the way I was. I had to accept that perfection did not exist. Accepting that meant that I was Pam perfect. I no longer had to measure my greatness with the world's ruler. I would never measure up by doing that. Being "Pam Perfect" meant that I was enough just the way I was. It was okay to take my cape off. It was okay not to make every meeting or game. It was okay for me to choose me. Choosing me was hard, but being alone while having a husband was hard. I chose my hard. I do not know if one day we will end up together. What I do know is that I will be complete. I did not realize how incomplete I was. Ironically, I thought the whole time I was miserable that I was hiding it from my kids. They knew the whole time. They were hiding it from me.

When you give 95 percent to the world and you only save five percent for yourself, you will always feel empty. You deserve to give yourself as much as you give others. I stopped seeing my therapist, but I still do my self-work. I live with intention. I learned I had to choose me every day. You have to choose you every day. If you do not stay prayed up and connected to the source, then you will allow the enemy to make you feel guilty.

Do not ever feel guilty for choosing to love you. I love to tell myself, you can't be a fan and an Olympian at the same time. Either you do the work every day and train to be the best version of yourself or you sit in the stands and cheer for everyone else. We all get 24 hours in a day. Use them with intention and start living with purpose. When I speak of this place, it's my peace. It's knowing that I had the courage to choose myself. This place, is a place that I will always choose. This place refers to happiness. I'm so in love with this place.

Spiritual Fruit

Colossians 3:14 - Clothe yourself in love. Love is what holds you all together in unity.

1 Corinthians 2:9 - No eye has seen the things God has prepared for those he loves.

Jeremiah 33:3 - Call unto me, and I will answer thee.

Corinthians 16:14 - Let all you do be done in love.

Speak Your Truth

Do not ever let the world make you feel like you cannot get help. Everyone needs somebody at least once in his or her life. Jesus had 12 disciples. If He needed people, please know that you will too! I took a chance on me. I decided that I wanted to start living and loving me. I wanted to start in this place. We always say, "Oh, next year I will start. When my children grow up, I will make time for me." No, honey, tomorrow isn't promised. Make a conscious effort to live your life in this place. My favorite quote states: The problem is we think we have time. What can you change? How can you start living your life intentionally and with purpose? What will it take to get you from "that place" to "this place"?

CHAPTER ELEVEN

Acceptance

People can't make you happy. That is a seed that must be planted, nurtured, and watered deep inside of you. Create your own smile.

Pamela Rawls

Acceptance

"Yes, honey, you look amazing!"

That is what I tell my clients as they look at themselves in the mirror. Outside of being a Cardiac Radiographer, I am also an Eyelash Artist. I love to lash because it makes women feel so beautiful. The sad part is that just about every woman that looks at herself in the mirror loves what I have done, but instantly points out her flaws. I can absolutely relate because I used to be the exact same way.

Why do we do this as women? Why do we feel the constant need to be perfect? We have allowed our self-value to come down to a "like". Social media is not an ideal way to measure your beauty...and neither is your mirror! Your beauty, real beauty, comes from within. It is who you are that determines your beauty. It really does not matter how fine you are right now, honey, gravity will win eventually.

I remember being extremely overweight. I had become comfortable in my discomfort. Just because you find yourself in a particular place in life does not mean that is where you belong or even where you have to stay. I hated myself. I would hide my food and eat in it in private. I did not need anyone to remind me that I was cheating on my billionth diet. I never felt beautiful. I always just felt okay. I learned at a very young age to be funny so that people would notice my humor and not my size. I decided to go on another diet shocker. First thing Monday morning it was on! This time I was really going to do it. To my surprise, I actually succeeded. Believe it or not, it still wasn't enough. I still was not happy. Even though I went from a size 20 to a size six, I still felt fat. I know you are saying, "Girl, please, a size six?!"

You see, it does not matter what the world thinks. It only matters what you think. I still did not feel good enough. Everyone thought I was crazy. Again, that did not matter. I worked out so hard trying to achieve this perfect body. I am still waiting for that perfect body to show up. Once I realized that my dream body was not coming, I woke up. I allowed myself to accept my flaws. It was through acceptance that I realized I was flawless. It wasn't the size of my jeans that made me beautiful; it was the size of my heart.

I have not read the entire Bible. I am in no way a Bible scholar, but I can guarantee you that thou shall have small thighs is not is the Psalms. Being flawless meant that I was enough. I did not have to get another "like" on a photo on social media. I did not have to measure up to the next top model. I decided that I was imperfectly perfect. Learning to love who I was, changed me. It took way more energy hating myself than it did to love me. I have stretch marks and scars. I love me. I have to.

Be mindful, you have to show people how to love and accept you. You can show them better then you can tell them. Accept yourself. And, yes, acceptance is so hard. If you can just be honest with yourself and allow yourself to be free from the opinions of others, it will liberate you. The strongest woman in the world is the one who does not need validation from anyone. Can you imagine waking up every morning loving what you see? You determine your day, not the world. Learn this positive affirmation; I AM ENOUGH. Perfection does not exist. I am HER! Say that every day until you believe it. Convince yourself and then take the time to convince the world. You have the power to change your life. It is all up to you to create the life that you want.

Our walk has come to an end. As you continue on your journey, I want you to identify your past. Accept what you cannot change and change what you cannot tolerate. Love the skin you are in and realize that this is your only life. I completely understand that trying to fly all the time is hard, but it beats walking! You have the power to make this life your best life. Look at yourself and say, "I am enough!" Perfection does not exist! I am her!

Spiritual Fruit

Ephesians 4:26 - Don't let the sun go down while you are still angry.

Isaiah 66:9 - I will not cause pain without allowing something new to be born.

Isaiah 14:27- All the forces of darkness cannot stop what God has ordained.

Joel-2:25 - I will restore.

Speak Your Truth

No one is happy all of the time. Happiness starts and ends with you. Define the word "happy" in your words. What does happiness look like to you? What is in your life that is pulling from your happiness and how can you fix it?

____

____

____

____

____

____

____

____

____

____

____

____

____

____

Final Thoughts to My Readers

Self-care is so important. It begins with you. This is something that should never end. If this makes you feel uncomfortable, then look at it this way. Self-care doesn't mean think of only you. It simply means, Me Too! You have to put you on your list.

I did a seminar a couple of years ago. It was the first time that I decided to fly. My daughter, who at the time was 9 ½ years old, said the most profound thing to me. "Momma, you should write down all of the places that you are going to go to. The world needs to hear you speak."

My response, "Honey, you're really sweet. I'm waiting on God."

She quickly responded, "Momma, you can't expect God to do everything! You have to do your part!"

I sat there in amazement. The seed that was placed in me placed a seed in me. She was absolutely right. Here I was waiting on God when God was waiting on me.

During the seminar, I made a profound request. List the five most important things in your life. Out of everyone in the room, only five chose to place themselves on their list! I realized, before you can be any good to anyone, you have to be good to you. You must do your Self-work. Do you love yourself? I mean like really love yourself. Can you look in the mirror and love what you see?

The reason I wrote this book was to help someone else. I wanted to be transparent so that I could let you know that you are not alone. Many women feel alone. A lot of them feel helpless and hopeless. I do not know a person who at times has not felt like giving up. You can turn it all around. You have to do some work, but you are worth the work! It all starts with self-care! Once you learn to pour into you, you will not have to worry and wait for the world to do it!

Learn to keep your own cup full. It is so easy to give to others. Why is that? Why do we never have trouble doing for others? Somehow, it becomes complicated to take care of ourselves or make ourselves a priority. You have to clap for you. You have to be your biggest cheerleader. Find some things that you love to do. Rediscover who you are and what you like. Take a hot bath and relax. Play your favorite music. Or you could take a beautiful walk in nature.

I learned a long time ago, if you sit around and wait for someone to clap for you...you will be waiting. I am not telling you that people will not pour into you. What I am saying is for you not to wait for them to pour. You control your space, time, and energy. Keep yourself balanced. Give and love on yourself. Teach the world how to treat you. Stop talking negatively about yourself. Speak life over your own life. Believe in God's promises. The word says that your latter will be greater. This is your season. Learn to take care of you. Make yourself a priority and not an option. Do something nice for yourself every day. Think about how much you give out every single day. It is necessary to save some of it for yourself. To thine own self be true. Whatever you acknowledge and do not change, you choose.

I challenge you to choose you. You are not choosing you to be selfish. You are choosing you because you matter! There are many types of apples in the world. Everyone has their particular choice to choose which type they like. It is usually something about the inside of a particular apple that wins people over. There are many types of apples and not one is perfect.

Remember, even the best apples have bruises…

About the Author

Pamela Rawls is a native of Paris, Kentucky. She graduated in 2006 with her Certification in Radiology and currently works as a Cardiac and Neurological Radiographer.

A proud mother of two, Pamela has always enjoyed having a relationship with Christ. She is a faithful member of the Centerville Missionary Baptist Church where she is a member of the choir, Women's President, Vacation Bible School teacher, and a Young Adult Sunday School Teacher. She truly believes that God has a special plan for us all. Writing this book has become one of her greatest accomplishments.

Learning to love yourself completely is the most important thing you can ever do. God is love. God is inside of you and He will never leave you. If you can master loving yourself, you can treat others with the respect that they deserve. Always remember, you have a voice. Speak your truth!

~ Pamela

9 780578 724829